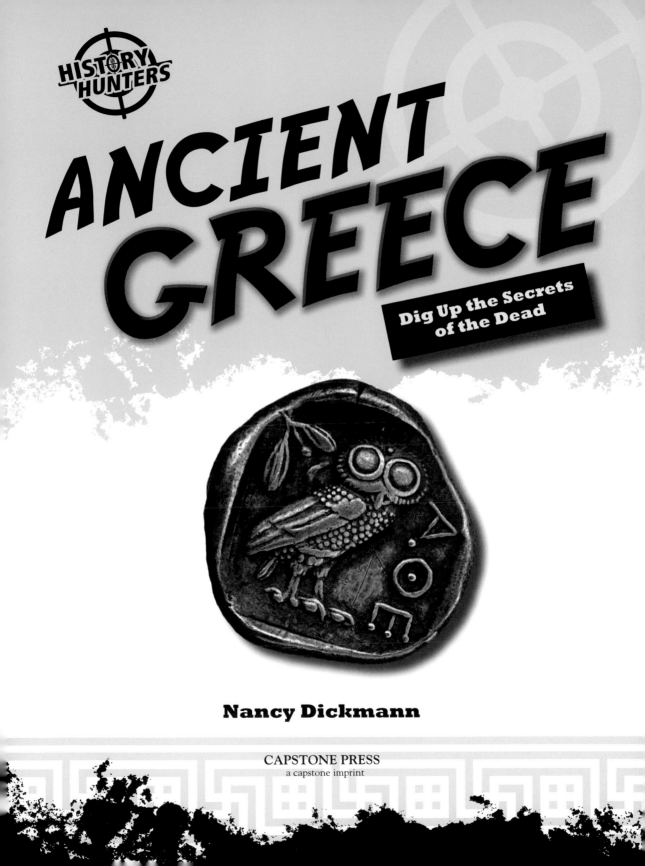

# HISTORY HUNTERS

# ANCIENT GREECE

## Dig Up the Secrets of the Dead

**Nancy Dickmann**

CAPSTONE PRESS
*a capstone imprint*

To contact Capstone Global Library please call 800-747-4992, or visit our web site
www.capstonepub.com

Produced for Capstone by Calcium
Edited by Sarah Eason and Jennifer Sanderson
Designed by Paul Myerscough
Picture research by Rachel Blount
Consultant: John Malam
Production by Paul Myerscough
Originated by Calcium Creative Limited © 2016
Printed and bound in China

20 19 18 17 16
10 9 8 7 6 5 4 3 2 1

**Library of Congress Cataloging-in-Publication Data**
Hardback ISBN 978 1 5157 2535 0
e-book ISBN 978 1 5157 2555 8

**Acknowledgments**
The author and publisher are grateful to the following for permission to reproduce copyright material:
Shutterstock pp. 4 (Vladimir Sazonov), 7 (Alexander A.Trofimov), 8 (Milosk50), 9 (AridOcean), 11 (Abxyz), 15
bottom (Luigi Nifosi), 16 (BlackMac), 18 (Anastasios71), 19 (Dermot68), 26 (Risteski Goce), 28-29 bottom
(V. J. Matthew), 29 right (Tracing Tea); Wikimedia Commons cover (Jebulon, National Archeological Museum,
Athens), pp. 1 (Marie-Lan Nguyen), 5 (Jebulon), 6 (Olaf Tausch), 10 (Sharon Mollerus), 12 (Jastrow), 13
(Jastrow), 15 top (Deutsches Museum, Munich, Germany), 17 (Marie-Lan Nguyen), 20 (Bibi Saint-Pol), 21
(Sharon Mollerus), 22 (Olecorre), 23 (Joanbanjo), 24 (Piot Collection, Marie-Lan Nguyen), 25 (Walters Art
Museum), 27 (Marie-Lan Nguyen).

Every effort has been made to contact copyright holders of material reproduced in this book. Any omissions will be
rectified in subsequent printings if notice is given to the publisher.

# CONTENTS

Throughout the book you will find Deadly
Secrets boxes that show an historical object.
Use the clues and the hint in these boxes to
figure out what the object is or what it was
used for. Then check out the Answer box at the
bottom of the page to see if you are right.

# ANCIENT GREECE

The country of Greece is surrounded on three sides by sea. It is made up of a **mainland** part and many islands. Greece is a modern nation and a popular tourist destination. However, 2,500 years ago, it was the center of a **civilization** whose influence is still felt today.

The first people to live in Greece's mountainous landscape arrived about 40,000 years ago. By about 3000 BCE, they had settled down in farming communities. They had learned how to make tools and weapons out of **bronze**.

**Archaeologist** Sir Arthur Evans excavated and reconstructed the ruins of the Minoan palace Knossos from the 1890s. Knossos is one of several Minoan palace sites.

Many beautiful **artifacts**, such as this gold mask, have been found at Mycenae.

## Minoans and Mycenaeans

The Minoan **culture** began in around 2000 BCE on the largest Greek island, Crete. The Minoans built **temples** and palaces. They traded with people all over the eastern Mediterranean Sea and North Africa. They painted pictures of daily life and developed a system of writing. In about 1600 BCE, a volcanic eruption, earthquakes, and a tidal wave struck the Minoans. Their civilization started to come to an end.

In about 1420 BCE, a new group of people took over on Crete. They were the Mycenaeans. They came from the mainland of Greece. They lived in small kingdoms that were each based around a walled city. One city was Mycenae, from where they get their name. The kingdoms often fought each other. The Mycenaeans traded throughout the Mediterranean and wrote down things.

## Dark Ages

The Mycenaeans were in decline by around 1100 BCE. Their cities were **abandoned**. Greece entered a period called the "Dark Ages," when nothing was written down. After 800 BCE, Greek culture started to revive. It came out of the Dark Ages and entered an exciting new time.

## Secrets of the Dead

### Minoan Writing

The Minoans on Crete developed a system of **hieroglyphic** writing that used pictures. Later they used writing called Linear A. The Mycenaeans adapted this to make their own writing, called Linear B. Linear B was **deciphered** in 1952. So far, no one has deciphered Linear A.

# DIGGING UP
## THE PAST

Although the ancient Greek civilization flourished long ago, we know a lot about the lives and ideas of the ancient Greeks. This is partly because many of their writings have been copied and passed down over the centuries. Archaeologists have also learned a lot by digging up the remains of ancient Greek cities, shipwrecks, and other sites.

Archaeologists have found a wide variety of artifacts. These include buildings such as temples and **amphitheaters**, grand statues, jewelry, and simple clay pots. Even a coin can give clues about life in the past. By analyzing what things are made of, scientists can often tell where they came from. This gives us information about ancient Greek trade.

## DEADly Secrets

This disk made of fired clay was found on Crete in 1908. Archaeologists think it was made sometime between 1850 and 1550 BCE. Can you guess what it was for?

**Hint:** You will have cracked the code if you figure it out.

# Shipwrecks

A lot of what we know about ancient Greek traders comes from shipwrecks found beneath the waters of the Aegean and Mediterranean Seas. Ships were one of the main ways of transporting goods, and the rocky coastline of Greece and its islands made shipwrecks common.

## A Living Culture

Today, some ancient Greek cities, such as Sparta, exist only as ruins. Others, like Athens, are still thriving. We use ancient Greek ideas in mathematics, science, and art. Our alphabet is based on the ancient Greek alphabet, and so are many of our words—even modern ones such as "telephone" and "microscope."

Stories from ancient Greece have been passed down, leading to reconstructions such as this version of the famous Trojan Horse.

Answer: No one really knows but most scholars believe that it is some form of writing. Although many have tried to decipher it, no one can agree on what it says. It might be a prayer, a list of foods or places, or even a song.

# CITY-STATES AND BITTER RIVALRIES

We talk about ancient Greece as a single civilization but it was not a unified country. Ancient Greek people shared the same culture, religion, and language but, after around 800 BCE, they were divided into independent **city-states**. A city-state was made up of a single city. Walls surrounded the cities to protect them from invaders.

The countryside around the city was also part of the city-state. The farms on this land would produce food to supply the people who lived in the city. The city at the center of a city-state usually had an area of high ground called an "acropolis," meaning "high city." The most important buildings were found at the Acropolis. Cities also had an open area called an agora. This was used as a marketplace.

The Acropolis in Athens includes a temple called the Parthenon. This was built as a home for the goddess Athena.

## Major City-States

The largest city-state was Athens. However, even at its height, it probably had a population of only a few hundred thousand people. Other major city-states included Corinth, Sparta, Megara, Thebes, and Argos.

## Rivalries

City-states sometimes fought wars against each other. One of the biggest conflicts was the Peloponnesian War. It was fought for 27 years from 431 to 404 BCE between Athens and Sparta. Each of these city-states had **alliances** with other city-states that fought on their side. Athens was richer and had a stronger navy. Sparta's army was more powerful. In the end, the Spartans won.

This map shows the location of some of the most important city-states in ancient Greece.

Thebes

Megara

Athens

Argos

Corinth

Sparta

## Secrets of the Dead

### Sparta: the Facts

- Sparta had two kings at a time: one to rule at home and the other to fight battles.
- Every male **citizen** had to become a full-time soldier.
- The men were always training for battle so they depended on slaves, called helots, to work the farms.
- Boys left home at the age of seven to go to military school. They were taught to be tough and resourceful.

# DEMOCRATIC VOTERS AND UNPOPULAR EXILES

In the early days, small groups of rich landowners or important men who had the people's respect governed many city-states. Occasionally, a single powerful man, called a tyrant, ruled the city-state. This was a system that worked for hundreds of years.

In Athens in 508 BCE, a nobleman named Cleisthenes introduced a new system. An assembly was set up in which every citizen could speak and vote on issues affecting the city. This new system was called "demokratia," a Greek word meaning "rule by the people." This is where the English word "democracy" comes from.

## DEADly Secrets

These small bronze tokens were found in Athens. Some have a solid middle and others have a hole. Can you think what they might be for?

**Hint:** Members of a **jury** would have used them.

## Trial by Jury

The Athenian legal system included trial by jury. Each jury had at least 200 men. Sometimes, juries had as many as 2,500 men. There was also a vote once a year. In this, any citizen could write the name of a person he wanted to get rid of on a piece of broken clay pot. The person who received the most votes had to leave Athens for 10 years.

Pericles was an extremely popular politician and general in Athens. He loved the arts, literature, and philosophy.

## Greek Democracy

Cleisthenes divided Athens's citizens into 10 groups, called tribes. Each one was named after a famous Athenian hero. Each tribe elected 50 representatives to a body called the "boule," which was like a council. The senate would propose laws. The assembly, consisting of all the citizens, would vote on them. The Athenian system was not quite the same as the one we use today. The only people who could join the assembly were citizens. Citizens were men over the age of 18 who were not slaves and who were born inside the city. Women, slaves, and men from outside the city could not take part.

Answer: A juror used these tokens to cast his vote on a case. A token with a solid middle meant innocent. A hole meant guilty. Each juror would drop a token into an urn and then the votes would be counted.

11

# FOOT SOLDIERS AND THE SPARTAN ARMY

Wars were common in ancient Greece. City-states often fought against each other in disputes over borders. However, in the early days of ancient Greece there was no real professional army.

Soldiers had to provide their own horses and weapons, so many of them were poorly armed. Most city-states had a policy of **drafting** all male citizens up to the age of 60, when there was a war. Some states had an elite professional unit but this was fairly small.

This painted vase shows two Greek soldiers using typical weapons and armor.

## Hoplites

By 650 BCE, a new type of foot soldier had developed. Called "hoplites," these men were better trained and well equipped. They all used similar weapons and armor. However, they were not a professional force. Hoplites often fought in a formation called a "phalanx." This meant standing in lines at least eight ranks deep. When they stood close together, half of one soldier's shield would protect the man to his left. They would walk toward the enemy, shouting a war cry, and holding long spears in front of them.

## Spartan Armies

Sparta was the exception to the rule. This city-state put military strength first. All male citizens over the age of 20 were members of a permanent army. They were tougher and better trained than most other soldiers. Many ancient Greeks said that in battle, one Spartan was worth several other men.

## DEADly Secrets

These bronze artifacts have images of Gorgons on them. Gorgons were legendary figures whose gaze turned people to stone. How do you think a hoplite might have used them?

**Hint:** A soccer player might find them useful, too.

## Secrets of the Dead

## A Hoplite's Equipment List

- Long wooden spear
- Short sword with bronze or iron blade
- Dagger
- Circular shield made of wood or leather
- Bronze helmet lined with leather
- Breastplate of bronze or leather
- Bronze greaves (shin guards)

Answer: These are greaves. Greaves were like shin guards and were worn to protect the hoplites' legs during battle.

# SAILING SHIPS AND DANGEROUS NAVIES

Much of life in ancient Greece revolved around the sea, and most people lived near the coast. The jagged coastline is full of inlets and natural harbors, and there are many islands. There were few roads crossing the rugged, mountainous terrain of the interior. It was much easier to travel by ship.

Traveling by ship may have been easier but it was still dangerous. Ships risked being attacked by pirates or damaged by powerful storms. Whenever possible, they sailed close to the shore to keep them from getting lost. Sometimes, this meant they ran aground on hidden rocks.

## Secrets of the Dead

### Parts of a Trireme Warship

- Seats for up to 170 rowers, arranged in three rows on each side
- Long oars for speed
- Long, narrow open deck for up to 30 armed hoplites, who could board enemy ships
- Bronze-covered **battering ram** for smashing into other ships
- All-seeing eyes painted onto the front of the ship
- Two large oars at the stern for steering
- Square sails for long journeys—the oars provided more speed
- No space for cargo so ships had to land each night for supplies

Battering ram

Painted eyes

# Shipwrecks

Archaeologists working underwater have found many wrecks of ancient Greek ships. These shipwrecks show us what Greek ships were like. One **merchant** ship had a hull made of pine and a mast made of spruce. The ropes for the square linen sail were made of flax or **hemp**. There were two large oars at the back for steering.

# Warships and Navies

Navies were important to Greek city-states, especially Athens. They were made up of fast, **maneuverable** warships. They had sails but they used oars in battle. Oars gave them extra speed and helped the boats turn quickly. The fastest type was called a trireme, with three rows of oars on each side. The main goal was to sink enemy ships by ramming them.

These pottery jars are called amphorae. They were used for storing and transporting olives, grain, oil, and wine. They have been found in many shipwrecks.

Square sail

Seats

Long oars

Open deck

Two large oars

# QUARRELING GODS AND POWERFUL BROTHERS

The ancient Greeks worshiped many different gods and goddesses. They believed that the gods could walk among people, and that each one controlled a different part of life.

The stories the ancient Greeks told about the gods were a way of trying to explain how the world worked. Most of the Greek gods were **related**. They quarreled, schemed, and fell in love with each other, just like ordinary people.

## Cities and Symbols

Many cities had patron gods and goddesses. The people of the city would worship these gods and goddesses so that the city and its people would be protected. To help people tell the gods apart, each one was shown with certain symbols. For example, Ares was the god of war, so one of his symbols was a spear. Athena's symbol was an owl, because she was the goddess of wisdom. Athena was the patron goddess of Athens.

Zeus was the father of some of the other gods, including Athena, Hermes, Apollo, and Ares.

## Three Brothers

Three of the most powerful gods were Zeus, Poseidon, and Hades. They were brothers who had divided up the world between themselves. Zeus was god of the sky (and king of all gods). Poseidon was god of the sea. Hades was god of the **underworld**, where people went after they died.

# DEADly Secrets

Each city-state issued its own coins. Can you guess which one this is from?

**Hint:** It shows the city's patron goddess.

## Secrets of the Dead

# Gods of Mount Olympus

These are the 12 main Greek gods, who lived on Mount Olympus:

- Zeus—king of the gods, god of the sky
- Hera—Zeus's wife, queen of the gods and the goddess of women
- Poseidon—god of the sea
- Demeter—goddess of farming
- Athena—goddess of wisdom
- Apollo—god of music and prophecy
- Artemis—goddess of the Moon and the hunt
- Ares—god of war
- Aphrodite—goddess of love
- Hephaestus—god of fire
- Hermes—messenger god
- Hestia—goddess of the **hearth** and home.

**Answer:** The coin is from Athens, which was named after the goddess Athena. She was the goddess of wisdom, which is why one of her symbols was the owl. Owls were thought to be wise.

# ELABORATE TEMPLES AND DAILY WORSHIP

The gods were powerful, so it was important to keep them happy. The ancient Greeks did this by building temples where the gods could be worshiped. Each temple's purpose was to be a home for a god or goddess.

Simple temples were often just a room with a statue of the god or goddess inside. The Greeks believed the god or goddess lived there. Later temples were bigger and more elaborate. They were made of stone and often had porches with rows of pillars at the front and back. The temples were decorated with carved or painted scenes. Some had a room that held valuable offerings.

The remains of many Greek temples still survive. This one, dedicated to Poseidon, lies to the south of Athens.

The Greeks asked questions of **oracles**, such as the famous one at Delphi. They hoped the oracles could reveal the future.

## Prayers and Offerings

Most ancient Greeks began the day with prayers. Many houses had their own **altars**. People would pour wine over the altar as an offering. They prayed to the gods that could help them the most. For example, if they were about to go on a journey, they would pray to Hermes, and if they were worried about their crops they would pray to Demeter.

## Gifts to Please the Gods

The ancient Greeks believed that the gods might be offended if they **sacrificed** the wrong type of animal as an offering, or prayed in the wrong way. For example, only female animals could be sacrificed to a goddess. People had to face east to pray to a sky god. Each god or goddess had his or her own priests. The priests made sure that the rules were followed. The ancient Greeks believed that reading signs or **omens** could help them understand the will of the gods.

## Secrets of the Dead

### Ways to Tell the Future

The ancient Greeks had different ways to predict the future:
- consulting an oracle, such as the priestess at Delphi who spoke for the god Apollo
- interpreting the flight patterns of birds
- inspecting the organs of animals after they had been sacrificed
- interpreting people's dreams
- looking at the positions of the stars and planets.

# FAMILY LIFE AND SCHOOLS FOR BOYS

Ancient Greek citizens were expected to marry and have children. This was so that there would be more citizens to carry on the work of the city-state. Fathers led families, and children were important. Most families favored sons over daughters.

One week after a baby was born, the child's parents would invite friends and family to celebrate. They would name the baby, and pray and make sacrifices for the child to have a happy, healthy life.

Music was important in ancient Greece, and some students would have learned to play instruments such as the lyre.

## A Difficult Start

Not all babies were welcomed into the world in a celebratory way. A father could reject a baby if it was a girl or if it was unhealthy. The baby might then be left in the wilderness to die. Other parents abandoned their children because they were too poor to support them. These babies may have been brought up as slaves.

## School

Boys from important families were sent to school. School started at the age of seven. At school, boys learned the skills they would need to lead and govern. They also learned reading, writing, and mathematics. Parents had to pay for school so many poor boys left school early. Richer boys might stay until the age of 18. They would learn to play musical instruments, recite poetry, speak in public, and read the writings of famous philosophers.

## DEADly Secrets

Children in ancient Greece had to learn some of the same things that children do now. This object is from a Greek home. Can you guess what it was used for?

**Hint:** You probably used one to go to the washroom as a toddler.

## Secrets of the Dead

### Women's Rights

Greek women had few rights. They had to do as their father or husband wished. Wealthy women did not work, but poor women usually worked. Spartan women had more rights than women in other areas. Girls would be taught skills, such as weaving and cooking, by their mothers.

Answer: This is a child's commode or potty. The child would sit in the top section with his or her legs sticking out of the opening at the front. The commode would be emptied when the child had finished.

# SIMPLE HOMES AND SORRY SLAVES

Many of the buildings that have survived from ancient Greece are grand public buildings such as temples and theaters. They were made of stone and built to last. Houses, which were built of mud brick, stone, and wood, have not survived. However, we know about Greek houses because archaeologists have found their remains.

## Ancient Greek Houses

Most houses were fairly small. They were built around a central courtyard. The roofs were made of clay tiles. The windows had no glass. Instead, they had wooden shutters to keep out the Sun. Most houses would only have one story, but richer families would have two. In these houses, the bedrooms were upstairs and the kitchen and living rooms were downstairs. There might also be a special room dedicated to Hestia, the goddess of the hearth. Women had a room where they could spin, weave, sew, and do other jobs.

This early bathtub is short. A person would have sat in it while a servant poured water over him or her.

This small artifact is made of clay. Many Greek homes would have had several of these. Can you guess what it is?

**Hint:** You would definitely need one to see at night. • • • •

## Keeping Clean

Only the grandest homes had bathrooms. Most people either used public baths or used a bucket or a stream for washing. They used a chamber pot instead of a washroom. It was hard work filling a bathtub so only people with slaves could enjoy this **luxury** at home. After a bath, people rubbed scented oil onto their bodies.

## Secrets of the Dead

### Slavery: the Facts

- Slaves were thought of as property.
- Most slaves were prisoners, captured in war.
- Slaves were bought and sold at slave markets.
- A rich family might have as many as 50 slaves. Poor families had slaves to help them with their work, too.
- Many slaves worked on farms and in homes. Some worked underground in mines or on ships.
- Slaves could not marry or have children without their owner's permission.

**Answer:** It is a small oil lamp. Oil was poured into the lamp through the hole at the top. Then a wick (made of string coated in wax) was placed in the spout and lit.

# WEARING CLOTHES AND GOING NAKED

Most ancient Greek clothes were very simple. They were made of wool, linen, or cotton. Summers were very hot, so clothes were often lightweight. The ancient Greeks wore strappy leather sandals or went barefoot. They wore hats for protection against the Sun.

The basic garment for a man was a **tunic**. Tunics were a little like long T-shirts. Young men usually wore knee-length tunics. Older men wore longer ones. Tunics could be worn with a belt. In cold weather, a man would wear either a long cloak called a "himation" or a short one called a "chlamys" over his tunic.

This statue shows a Greek woman wearing a chiton and himation.

## Secrets of the Dead

### Going Naked

Clothes were not always necessary for men in ancient Greece. The ancient Greeks admired the natural beauty of the human body. In these situations it was acceptable for men to go naked:

- at private men-only parties, called symposia, where they ate and talked together
- during exercising or competing in sports, especially at the Olympic Games
- at a public **bathhouse**.

# DEADly Secrets

This artifact is made from bronze and would have belonged to a wealthy woman. The bronze on the inside was once highly polished. Can you guess what she would have used it for?

**Hint:** You might look into something similar but yours will be made of glass.

## Women's Clothes

Most women wore a long, simple robe called a "chiton." It was belted. Brooches were used to make armholes. Over their chitons women wore "himations." Most women knew how to spin and weave their own clothes. Dyes were expensive, so most people had clothes in natural colors. It was fashionable to have pale skin in ancient Greece. It showed the woman was rich enough not to have to work in the fields and get a tan. Women would often powder their faces with chalk to make them pale. Some even used white lead, which we now know is poisonous.

Answer: This is a compact mirror. Glass-making was a new skill and it was very expensive. No one yet knew how to make mirrors of glass backed with metal, so they used polished bronze instead.

# BASIC BREAD AND HUNTING BEASTS

Most ancient Greeks lived by farming. However, good farmland was hard to find in some places. In rocky, mountainous areas, people kept animals, such as goats and sheep, rather than planting crops.

The **staples** of the Greek diet were bread and porridge. These were usually made from wheat or barley. For breakfast, Greeks would eat fruit and bread dipped in wine. They ate more bread at lunch. They also ate cheese, eggs, and a wide range of fruits, vegetables, nuts, and beans.

## Flavoring Food

Fresh herbs were used to flavor food, and honey was used to sweeten it (the ancient Greeks did not know about sugar). Olives were an incredibly important crop. The ancient Greeks squeezed olives to make olive oil. Olive oil was used for cooking, for burning in oil lamps, and for keeping people's skin clean and soft.

Olives are still an important crop in Greece today.

The man in this vase painting is hunting a deer.

## Fish and Meat

Although Greece is surrounded by the sea, the waters did not have a reliable year-round stock of fish. The ancient Greeks liked fish but it was fairly scarce and hard to keep fresh. They often pickled it to use as a relish on bread. Fish could also be salted to preserve it. The ancient Greeks raised pigs and chickens for their meat but only rich people could afford to eat meat regularly. Sheep and goats were kept for milk as well as for their wool and hides (skins).

## Secrets of the Dead

### Hunting: the Facts

- Most Greeks hunted for food but rich men often hunted for pleasure.
- There are many **myths** and legends about heroes hunting.
- Rabbits, hares, deer, and wild boar were all hunted.
- Weapons used by the ancient Greeks included nets and traps, spears, or bows and arrows.
- Some ancient Greeks hunted on horseback. Many used dogs.

27

# ARTS, SPORTS, AND A LASTING LEGACY

Music was popular in ancient Greece, especially at parties. At parties, guests might recite poetry. Entertainers might sing or play musical instruments. Some forms of entertainment took place in the home and others were part of large, public festivals.

Greek men enjoyed competing in sports such as wrestling, boxing, discus, javelin, and running. Sporting competitions were often held as part of religious festivals. The Olympic Games were the most famous. They were held every four years at Olympia. Men competed in the Olympic Games. A separate competition for women, called the Heraean Games, was held. In Sparta, women were allowed to take part in athletic competitions, too.

## Secrets of the Dead

### Greek Theater: the Facts

- Ancient Greek theater probably started as part of a religious festival. Over time, it evolved into an art form.
- Plays were usually either **tragedies** with a moral message or **comedies** that sometimes made fun of politicians or other important people.
- Plays were performed in open-air amphitheaters.
- Only boys and men could perform on the stage.
- The actors wore masks to show who their character was and what their emotions were.
- Some masks were reversible, with a calm expression on one side and an angry one on the other.

# DEADly Secrets

These small items are bones from the ankle of a sheep. Ancient Greek children and adults would have enjoyed playing with them. How do you think they were used?

**Hint:** A similar game is still played today with a bouncy ball and jacks.

The largest theaters could hold more than 18,000 spectators.

## Lasting Legacy

Today, the Olympic Games are held every four years. Plays written by ancient Greek authors are still performed. A lot of our culture and language is based on ideas from ancient Greece. Archaeologists have made many discoveries that teach us about this fascinating culture and there is still so much more to discover.

Answer: These bones are often called "knucklebones," and they were thrown in a game very similar to the modern game of jacks. There were several different versions of the game, with different rules. Knucklebones could sometimes be made of glass or metal.

# GLOSSARY

**abandon** desert, leave alone

**alliance** union between people or states to achieve a goal

**altar** table or surface used for a religious ritual

**amphitheater** outdoor theater

**archaeologist** person who digs up and studies the remains of ancient cultures

**artifact** object made by a human being that has cultural or religious importance

**bathhouse** public building where people can go to exercise and get clean

**battering ram** large beam used to break down walls or doors, or to make a hole in the side of a ship

**bronze** strong metal made from a mixture of melted metals, such as copper and tin

**citizen** free man who had the right to participate in the government of his city-state

**city-state** independent state made up of a city and the land surrounding it

**civilization** society, culture, and way of life of a particular area

**comedy** drama that is humorous

**culture** ideas, beliefs, values, and knowledge shared by a particular group of people

**decipher** understand or interpret

**draft** call to the army

**hearth** floor of a fireplace, or the stone or brick area in front of it

**hemp** tall herb mainly grown in Asia

**hieroglyphic** writing system based on pictures that represent a word, part of a word, or a sound

**jury** group of people who listen to the facts of a legal case and decide its outcome

**luxury** something that is part of living a rich and comfortable life

**mainland** land that is part of a continent and not an island

**maneuverable** easy to move

**merchant** trader or salesperson

**myth** traditional story that tries to explain why the world is the way that it is

**omen** sign from the gods that warned of good or evil to come

**oracle** message given by a god or goddess. It can also mean the priest or priestess who delivered the message, or the sacred place where it happened

**related** from the same family

**sacrifice** kill an animal or person to please a god in a religious ceremony

**staple** something that is important because it is used every day

**temple** building where gods and goddesses are worshiped

**tragedy** drama in which the main character falls to disaster

**tunic** simple garment made from two rectangles of cloth stitched together and tied with a belt

**underworld** imaginary world of the dead, somewhere beneath Earth

# READ MORE

## Books

Burns, Kylie. *Sparta!* (Crabtree Chrome). New York: Crabtree, 2013.

Catel, Patrick. *What Did the Ancient Greeks Do for Me?*
(Linking the Past and Present). North Mankato, MN: Heinemann, 2011.

Meyer, Susan. *The Totally Gross History of Ancient Greece* (Totally Gross History).
New York: Rosen Central, 2016.

Nardo, Don. *Daily Life in Ancient Greece* (Daily Life in Ancient Civilizations).
North Mankato, MN: Heinemann, 2015.

## Web Sites

This web site has an interactive map and a quiz about the ancient Greeks:
**www.dkfindout.com/us/history/ancient-greece**

If you want to learn more about the ancient Olympic Games, visit this site:
**www.librarypoint.org/ancient_olympic_games**

Learn 10 key facts about the ancient Greeks:
**www.ngkids.co.uk/history/10-facts-about-the-ancient-greeks**

This site includes a timeline and links to other interesting information
about ancient Greece:
**www.timeforkids.com/destination/greece/history-timeline**

# INDEX